GW00671579

IN A HARE'S EYE

Breda Wall Ryan

Doire Press

First published in March 2015

Doire Press
Aille, Inverin
Co. Galway
www.doirepress.com

Layout & cover design: Lisa Frank
Author photo: Eamon Wall
Cover image: *Spring Clean* by Sarah Majury
www.sarahmajury.co.uk

Printed by Clódóirí CL
Casla, Co. na Gaillimhe

ISBN 978-1-907682-36-0

We gratefully acknowledge the assistance of The Arts Council / An Chomhairle Ealaíon.

ACKNOWLEDGEMENTS

Versions of some of these poems have appeared in the following journals and anthologies: *Mslexia, And Other Poems, Southword, Skylight 47, The Weary Blues, Deep Water Journal, The Workshop Anthology, Spinoza Blue, Revival, Poetry 24, Orbis, The Galway Review, Poets Meet Painters, Windows Authors & Artists Introductions Series 10, Fish Anthology, ESOF Science Meets Poetry 3, Blue Fifth Review / The Blue Note, Crannóg, The Rialto, Outburst Magazine* and *The Ofi Press Magazine.*

Sincere thanks to the judges of competitions in which poems have been placed or won, especially the iYeats Poetry Competition, Poets Meet Painters Competition, Dromineer Literary Festival Poetry Competition and Over the Edge New Writer of the Year Competition, 2013; RSPB / The Rialto Nature Poetry Competition and Fool for Poetry Chapbook Competition, 2014; Patrick Kavanagh Awards 2013 and 2014; and the Gregory O'Donoghue International Poetry Prize, 2015.

'Wake' references fragments of Seamus Heaney's poetry engraved on the Poet's Walk in The Devil's Glen, Ashford, Co. Wicklow.

My thanks to Poetry Ireland Introductions Series, 2014; Windows Publications Authors & Artists Introductions Series 10 and Stinging Fly / Irish Writers' Centre Summer Reading Series for selecting me as a featured poet; to my colleagues in Hibernian Poetry and Green Kite Writers for their support and inspiration; to Damian Smyth and Paul Perry for their close reading and suggestions on earlier manuscripts; to Lisa Frank and John Walsh at Doire Press; to Sarah Majury; and to my family, friends and fellow poets who accompany me on my poetry journey. Thank you all.

CONTENTS

I. In a Hare's Eye

Self Portrait as She Wolf   11

You Don't Need Light to Find Your Way in Your Own House   12

Self Portrait in the Convex Bulge of a Hare's Eye   13

Dear Surgeon, I imagine you   14

Vanishing   15

Brighid's Eve, Intensive Care   16

Knots   17

The Room   18

Portrait of the Artist's Mother as a Merlin   20

Woman of the Atlantic Seaboard   22

Remnants   24

The Camel, Perfected   25

Salt   27

Jael's Testimony   28

Dumbstruck   30

To Paul, a Refutation   31

Dreamless   32

The Second Wife's Tale   34

Three Sisters   36

The Stranger's House   37

Cailín Rua   38

The Fisherman's Song to the Mermaid   40

The Dream of the Fisherman's Wife   42

Watching Alice   43

The Snow Woman   44

II. Landmarks

Walking from the Square to the West Lodge Hotel, Bantry in   47
a Heatwave

A Map of Getting Lost   48

New York Fire Escape   49

Traces   50

Missing   51

Birch Tree Grove   52

Wake   53

Inheritors   54

Landmarks   57

Miracle   58

Grushie   59

From Céide Fields: 61

        (i) Stone Song   61

        (ii) The Inkling   62

        (iii) Becoming the Ancestor   64

        (iv) The Laying of the Bog   65

        (v) South of Erris   66

Homecoming   67

Haiku Sequence from The Farmhouse, Wicklow   68

Horse Stance   69

If What is, is Other   70

Tremolo   71

Glimpsed   72

Silver Birches   73

Naming the Boat   75

Summer's End   77

The Furnock   78

About the Author   79

For Jerry Ryan,
my most stalwart champion

I. In a Hare's Eye

Self Portrait as She Wolf

You sheer away from the warm,
many-tailed beast,
spurn the communal dream.

Beyond the shelter of pine and fir
you lope across open ground
where cold scalds your lungs,

feel a soft-nosed bullet's kiss,
lick the salt wound clean,
almost drown in a starry bog,

but break through its dark mirror,
meet your reflection
in a boutique window on a city street

among mannequins in ersatz furs,
the last of your kind,
or the first.

Only look back once,
for a silhouette, a hungry scent.
There is still time to re-trace your spoor,

answer the tribal howl. Your throat opens
on one long, swooped syllable,
almost a word.

You Don't Need Light to Find Your Way in Your Own House

You sound your way by the creak of bedsprings forgetting
          your shape, feet slapping floorboards,
     the dry screech of the door-hinge.
Counterpoint to your body's tides,
       not far off the ocean pounds the seawall.

What woke you? A trans-Atlantic's fibrillations
         muffled in cloud? The storm's growl
     in the chimney-throat? Asphalt hisses
at wet tyres, an engine slows; you follow
      its purr to the end of the road.

Your hand whispers to the banister rail;
        ahead of their echo, footsteps tap on stairs,
     the loose board backfires. You look for the moon;
rain on the skylight patters and slides.
      What woke you? Inside or out? Sleepsounds

roll from a high window. You rattle the locks,
       dodge the motion sensor,
     choose to stay in the dark. A blackbird's startle
jolts the hair on your neck.
      A dustbin clatters — man or fox? Fear is a pulse.

The socket fizzes when you plug the kettle in,
        the fridge coughs, then settles to a steady hum.
     Three sharp snaps light the gas, you bang
a pan on the stove, milk hisses and spits.
      Away in the distance, a dying alarm chirps.

You reach for the coffee jar, clang a spoon on the sink.
        New wire in your sternum twangs
     like a banjo string. A face at the window:
doubled in glass, your own reflection
      amplifies nightsounds. You don't need light.

Self Portrait in the Convex Bulge of a Hare's Eye

My first word for Hare was *cailleach*,
witch or crone, slack-skinned
hag with blade-edged bones.

I met her again today
where seven hare-sisters grazed
a scrawny field at Renvyle,

face to face inhaled her lepus breath,
gazed through my shadow-face
cupped in her glass-dark eye.

'Which is my animal shade?' I asked
the coven of leathern-ears.
Each licked her cloven lip and chanted,

'I', 'I', and 'I'. Hare with sea-salt tongue
rolled the dark bulge of her eye,
answered, 'All of us, all of us here;

we show no map of your journey, we
are you when you get there.'
I grabbed at scut and slippery ear,

begged her to tell more
but rain rolled in from Boffin,
plump drops slicked her fur,

she twitched a salt-crusted whisker,
slipped into Otherwhere
like a white horse in *ceo draíochta*,

left me straddling a barbed wire fence
with two handfuls of loose belly-skin
and a jagged gash in my thigh.

Dear Surgeon, I imagine you

sliding the metal ring off your fingertip,
stitching it into the pulp of my heart.
The X-ray's a glimmer of heart gone pear-shaped,
and I'd like to know, when it all goes wrong,
when the flaps on the new valve flutter like mad,
helpless to open or close as they should,
when you slice the mis-shapen lump,
instead of grafting metal to old rootstock,
could you sow one black pip from a pear?
Let it grow to a tree, let the fruit ripen and swell,
then leave it to blet in the crimson dark
till it runs with sweetness and juice.
I don't trust your steel ring or your knife
but a Conference Pear is a keeper, for life.

Vanishing

They take your name

tag your wrist
birth date
gender
unique number

They note your history

take your clothes
issue a paper gown
towel
disinfectant

They send you to the showers

drip chemicals
where blue vein
bisects
indigo X

They write up your chart

cocktail
dose
toxicity
effect

They take your hair.

Brighid's Eve, Intensive Care

That night I sailed the Islets of Langerhans,
my spinnaker bellied by ionic wind,
rats scavenged casks among the strakes
and fought for purchase on the rigging overhead.
The crew craved rations of Jamaica rum,
molasses, treacle, even bee-laced grog.

Starved ravings edged me overboard,
I dived below the phosphorescent seas,
swam salty underwaters raw as blood —
without a sextant, who could tell the way?
Light oscillated from uncharted stars,
the moons were cobalt, wandering overhead.

Brighid hauled me back on board,
pried open my clenched teeth
and placed the lost electron on my tongue
to summon Panacea and Akeso.
They rafted flotsam from the fevered ship
into a *naomhóg* bound with Brighid's band

lashed fast in double Carrick bends,
unfurled a square sail from her healer's cloak,
then hitched her rushy cross to be our mast.
While Panacea pinned me to the deck,
Akeso helmed us through Delirium Straits,
twisted serpents into oars and rowed ashore.

A trickle of pure oxygen at my ear
and psychotropic histories in my head,
I spent the dog watch on the coral sand.

Knots

The day before, I asked the butcher
for a cow's heart, intact, to study how it works.
He pointed with a knife-tip to aorta, mitral valve,
pulmonary vein, superior vena cava, ran water
through to show its pumping action.

He tied the bloody package to take home,
a flick-snap knot it took a blade to open,
said a heart op. is not rocket science,
a good surgeon can do a dozen before breakfast,
eyes shut, one hand behind his back.

I think mine did. His sutures slipped.
He says we must go in again.
Mr Surgeon, learn to tie a butcher's knot.
And this time, please, don't even blink.

The Room

When you came back with the swallows
for summer, our mother was gone.

Our children swung in the beech,
swallows quartered the sky,
their squeals pierced her room.

I heard you ease open her door
as I used to after the burial.

You stood quite still, inhaled
faded scents: detergent, dust,
Palmolive soap, our mother's skin.

Crocheted daisies printed your cheek,
memory hurting the gap in your heart.

Springs creaked, you got to your feet,
tugged sheets into hospital corners,
tried to restore what was broken.

It stayed awry. You finger-tipped
her nightgown, rosary, Kalil Gibran,

Birds of the British Isles.
Bureau drawers slid out and in,
doors groaned. I heard you find

what I found months before:
she got rid of every stitch before the end,

except her Sunday skirt, good winter coat,
lambskin gloves, and — so out of character —
that pretty satin slip.

Surely she had left a message
for her favourite with your quarter-century

of letters gaudy with African stamps?
Her writing box clattered, shocked
the silence with its emptiness.

All that summer's still afternoons
you searched mattress, hems, page margins

until swallows gathered
in coded sequences on telephone wires
and Africa called you home.

Before you left I swore
she left no message. I was wrong —

she left her emptied room.

Portrait of the Artist's Mother as a Merlin

I woke once to a cold house.
We were snow-bound, running low
on wood and cow-nuts, and out of cocoa.
It was my task to warn my mother
when the fire burned low. And perhaps
I wanted her hands to gentle my hair
into braids and comfort the baby,

and so I went outside and called her name
in cowyard, barn and across the blank fields,
and heard the dead silence of snow.
I came on her out of sight of the house,
perched on a weathered, broken chair,
steam rising about her in a cloud,
her enormous green eyes

fixed on a fresh-killed hen she clutched
by its claws. Her left hand plunged
the carcass in a steaming bucket,
and the hand that stirred soup
and soothed the baby stripped feathers
from the breast and dropped them
onto the snow.

From my corner of the yard
I watched her white breaths,
her hands tearing feathers from flesh,
flurries of down drifting
around her head like bloodied snow,
catching on straws and the barbs
of blackthorns.

I was very young, made anxious
by overheard talk of ruin
and hunger and a long winter,
and it helped that day to know
that out of sight of the nest,
my mother became a wild thing,
a merlin at her plucking post.

Woman of the Atlantic Seaboard

You might meet her anywhere on the coast:
at Moher she is Rosmari, walks the high cliffs,
away from the busses and tour guides,
her face turned towards the west, sea in her hair.
Or at Renvyle, where a white carved stone
remembers the unbaptised, as Maighdean Mara,
she keeps vigil where the sea stole
their bones from the shore.

Call her Atlantia, she who waits in the lee
of a sea wall at Vigo for the boats to come in.
She looks deep into fishermen's eyes,
as if eyes can give back what they've seen,
a waterlogged husband, brother's shin bone,
a son's lobster-trap ribcage to carry home
in a pocket of her yellow oilskin.
Enough for a burial.

She is Marinella on Cabo Espichel, Morwenna
in Wales. Among wild women who comb
blueberry barrens in Maine she is Maris,
her fingers long as the sea's ninth wave,
stained from plucking sharp fruit in sea fog.
Find her on shore where Connemara ponies
ride out the surf. Take her home,
give her the stranger's place at the hearth:

she won't stay. Inland, she adds salt to her bath,
boils potatoes in seawater down to a salt crust.
Feed her dilisk and Carrigeen moss; she can't help
but return to the waves, to kelp and ozone.
She is Muirghein, born of the sea, the sea
salts her blood. Or call her Thalassa, mother
of Kelpies, Selkies, fin-flippered sea-mammals,
neoprene-skinned fish-hunters, creatures of the tide.

All lost to her. Oceania the seafarer's daughter,
sister, mother, wife; on a widow's walk in Boston,
she scans the horizon for a floater or a boat.
Meet her on the brink of the ocean, alone, winter
seas in her eyes. Call her by any of her names:
she will turn from you to the blue nor'wester,
shake brined beads from her hair. She will wait
for her drownlings forever, standing in the salt rain.

Remnants

An Old-Spiced, Gauloise hint
clings to the weft and warp
of this quilt

pieced from off-cuts scissored
from aeroplane-collared shirts,
psychedelic prints,

candle-wax batiks like rain-spatter
from a clear blue sky,
a silk tie-dyed maxi skirt,

a summery top gauzy as fog
from the Dandelion Market.
Its folds scatter old incense:

our shared tent on the Isle of Wight,
the Rathmines bedsit,
his skin-scent, the throb

of a tender blue vein at his temple,
'Nights in White Satin',
all the moody blues.

The Camel, Perfected

God's wife rose on the eighth day and looked upon creation. She beheld the camel and saw that it was an abomination. She called her servant and said: Go forth into the marketplace, and bring unto me all that the scrap merchants have gleaned after God created the universe. And the servant brought them. Then she went into the past, present and future and gathered all the sounds that wandered the four winds, and the echoes thereof. And God's wife created the horse.

Now when God awoke from his day of rest, he beheld the camel his wife had made, and rebuked her saying, What in all My names availeth a camel without hump or footpads? And she answered, This is my beloved horse. In him I am well pleased.

Then God said, What is a horse? And she answered,

What is a horse?
His head is a leather sound-box,
his ear, a fur purse for whispers,
his nose, a velvet lining for rich pockets,
his teeth are Taureg tent pegs,
his eyes are tar-bubbles.

His whicker is a wind-fluttered window-blind,
his whinny, a demisemiquavery descending scale on a trumpet,
his breath, a gust from a stoked furnace.

His walk is the weary march of late-shift miners,
his gallop, the rhythmic banging of a hundred drums,
his prance, the last raindrops wrung from a summer cloud.

His lungs are the bellows of a poor chapel harmonium,
his belly is a Beduoin's bundle,
his back, Ali Baba's carpet,
his withers, the wellsprings of angelwings,
his urine is pungent Pu-Erh tea from China.

His hind hooves are thunderclaps,
his fore-hooves, the beat of a rain-begone dance round a campfire,
his pastern bones are rhythm-sticks,
his cannonbones are Zulu knobkerries,
his coffinbones are snuffboxes.

His fetlocks are the swaying grass skirts of Nubian maidens,
his mane is young barley racing the wind,
his tail, a shoal of elvers swimming upriver,
his farts are giant puffballs.
If he had hands — Oh, if only he had hands!

Salt

"But his wife looked back from behind him, and became a pillar of salt."

(Genesis 19.26)

He'd tired of me as wife, disrespected
me before God's wise-guys, instructed me
on how to offer hospitality
as if I was his maid. I'd seen how he lusted

for our daughters, offered them to men of Sodom.
I stood between him and his base desire
but he bedded both when they reached Zoar,
then blamed the wine, claimed the girls led him on.

God's angels set me up so Lot would be restored
to singledom. I breathed smoke, smelt brimstone,
my little home dragged my heartstrings till I turned.

What woman worth her salt could resist?
Lot licked my snapped-off finger to check taste,
packed me in a sack so I won't go to waste.

Jael's Testimony

(Pedro Núñez del Valle. *Jael and Sisera*. c.1820, National Gallery of Ireland)

I

Hearing a man blunder into the guy ropes,
I hurried from the inner chamber, unveiled,
my hair unbound, to welcome
Heber, my husband, from the battlefield.
Finding Sisera, the Canaanite general, at the awning,
I begged him to turn aside and come into my tent.
I prepared a place for him, unbuckled his sword,
and covered him with a rug where he lay,
the blood of battle on him — not Heber's, I prayed.
I bathed his wounds with myrrh and aloes;
anointed him with camphire and spikenard.

He asked for water. Sweet milk I gave him,
beastings from my new-calved cow,
flavoured with calamus and cinnamon,
valerian and soporific spices.
My hand dripped with frankincense,
and my fingers with sweet-smelling myrrh,
honey and milk were under my tongue.
With words and welcomes I deceived him,
caused him to sleep with herbs and spices.
I saw he was well-wrought, in breastplate
and greaves he resembled my husband.

Then I closed my heart against pity.
I lifted the mallet high over my head
and brought it down on the head
of the tent peg, and drove the spike
into his temple behind his eyes.
It pierced his head as cleanly as a ripe pomegranate;
the bone splintered like the shell of a plover's egg.
His eyes flew open, as if taken by surprise;
and I said no word, but raised the mallet once more
and drove the spike home
and clinched his head to the earthen floor.

II

At last Heber has come home, weary from the battle.
With the corpse of his enemy I welcomed him.
The Judges also have entered the tent;
their accusations are like hornets
trapped under a vessel. I have broken the taboo,
tools and weapons being proper only
to the hands of men. But I tell those begrudgers,
'The mallet and spike are for setting up the tent;
and is that not woman's work?
Therefore they are chattels. Sisera is felled
in accordance with your laws.'

The people of Israel go up to the temple,
they offer to Yahweh an ox and a fatted lamb,
at all the watering places they sing
the triumphs of the Lord. Yet all gods are capricious,
they change sides on a whim.
Was it not Baal, god of thunder and deluge,
who mired Sisera's chariots, turned aside his spears
from the armies of Israel?
Therefore I shall go in secret to Baal's brazen altar,
lead to the sacrifice my beloved yellow calf,
for woman must do hard things to protect her hearth;

she must strengthen her hand
though her enemy resembles her husband,
and slaughter her favourite beast.
When men make war, woman must shift for herself.
Musicians sing my praises; I paid in shekels
for the psalm that is carried on the wind:
        'Most blessed of women be Jael,
            the wife of Heber the Kenite,
                of tent-dwelling women most blessed.'
Ye gods, harden my heart,
the bawling of my yellow calf is a blade in my ear.

Dumbstruck

Even our languages fail us,
blasted into silence,
nouns gutted of meaning,
Lie twisted to *Mental Reservation*,
titles defiled: *Father*, *Athair*,
Reverend split open,
the wormy antonym coiled in its core,
blind eye turned
to the rot in its heart.
Sanctuary violated,
superlatives we counted on torn
from their roots,
verbs hard-tempered in fire
spun to cloud by their mouths.
We cry out for reformation,
for pages of revelations nailed
to cathedral doors
in Dublin, Ferns, Cloyne.
They answer with pleas
of innocence in pulpit voices,
garbed like *toreros* in *trajes de luces*,
steel concealed
beneath silken embroideries.
Our strongest words fall defenceless
as Samson shorn of his hair:
we howl of unspeakable deeds,
peel the skin off our tongues,
burn them with new adjectives.

To Paul, a Refutation

"It is better to marry than to burn." (1 Corinthians 7.9)

When I have buried my husband, said the wife,
and wept to the moon,
I'll take the brush with the dented back
and unravel the knots in my hair,
splash my face and hands with water,
walk out in high heels.

I'll direct the police to the *Museo de Brujas*
where I'll give them a guided tour,
show how the spikes inside the Iron Maiden
compare with my old wounds,
invite them to test the thumbscrews
on my unsocketed bones.

Wearing careful grey cashmere and high collar,
I'll steady my nerve with red wine
and wait among the instruments of torture,
evidence of what women make men do.
I'll write what was dictated:
it is better to marry?

They'll arrive with shrieking sirens,
smell the petrol and roasting smoke.
By then I'll be ash, floating.
In ten years' time or a thousand,
they'll know ash knows no locks or borders;
it is better to burn.

Dreamless

A million crawling things run spiderwise
inside her skin, her skeleton is glass,
she needs another hit, and fast,

her skin is needle-tracked, she works
the street for heroin to stop the spiderlings,
she does a punter in a dash against a fence

and scores a thirty-second rush,
glass splinters in her veins fuse
into a waterfall of raindrops,

magic light spills from her fingertips,
she's blissed out, dreaming weightless while
the good brown horse outruns her dream,

she's goofing now, slumped outside a church,
between her knees a paper cup she holds out
like a sacred heart to passers-by,

small change spills through her fingertips
but not enough, another stranger in a car
earns her more dreams, she sucks her tongue

for spit to swallow fear, swears
on the Sacred Heart that she'll get clean,
then mugs the punter with a syringe,

again the spiderlings criss-cross her skin
and crawl inside her arm-tracks,
two blow-jobs on her knees to get a high,

she cooks the gear, a bag of china white,
loads up a syringe, smacks a vein, ties off
and hits; her hopes are answered with *amen*,

the dragon's knocked brown sugar girl
off her horse, the fall has sucked out
all her breath, her eyes are pinned,

she feels no crawly things, she has no skin,
her bones are glass, her heartbeats trickle
from her fingertips like raindrops when

the rain's about to stop...

The Second Wife's Tale

I wanted his gold at my throat, wanted
        Lir's mouth-filling tongue filling mine.
I sooted my lashes, red-berried my lips, smiled
        till my jaw cracked and went on smiling,
my breath wild mint at his ear, my hand a bird on his thigh.

        He married my sister.
When she died, a great whinging like swans
        swelled the silence inside me.
Four children pined for their mother, Lir for his wife.
        I'm no mother. No matter; I soothed Lir's wife-ache.
           This was my sorrow.

The river flows both ways,
        she carries away what she can take,
man or woman or child not grown to reason.
        She turns at the moon's demand,
her freshened waters full of the swimming
        of white swans, glass eels, sea trout, salmon.

I come from the littoral, water shaped me,
        men danced for my notice.
Lir made me second wife, I who was riverweed,
        he thought I had not a mean bone in my body.

        This is the second sorrow:
four wedges between me and my husband.
        I lured Lir's children to water,
left them to float as waterfowl.
        I am Aoife, mean through to the marrow.

When you speak of Lir's cygnets,
        tell of my punishment,
banished to winter nine hundred years.

Say winter's cold was her only dread,
now she's frozen to her marrowbones.

     Say ice grows where she holds her breath,
her voice is in the north wind's teeth,
     when she breathes the blizzard shrieks.
Say swans go swaddled in feathers and down
     but Aoife has only her own fine skin
between her flesh and the bitter wind.
     This is the greatest sorrow.

Three Sisters

Whip-graft my floating rib to a spur of the quicken tree
so my spirit endures as strong as the day I was born,
for I must destroy the destroyers of Bella, Donna and me.

Bella was fifteen and skilled in the remedy
for the man's complaint. For her healing hand she was burned
but I spliced her wish-bone to a spur of the quicken tree.

Gossips said good sister Donna left wifing for witchery,
damned her as Devil's whore when she bore the six-fingered bairn.
I raked the pyre for her bones. Burners of Bella and Donna knew me

as mild. The youngest. A child. I smiled, hid my ferocity.
Seducers, goodwives, magistrates came to strange harm
while I tended my sisters on the stock of the quicken tree,

threaded rosaries of devil's cherry to garland each nursery.
Shrank men's acorns to sloes. Stilled babes in the womb.
Destroyers of Bella and Donna, you almost destroyed me,

but on Bonfire Eve a six-fingered boy set me free
with tincture of nightshade and yew seed in wychbane tea.
He grafted my floating rib to a spur of the quicken tree;
now we three unite as destroyers: Bella, Donna and me.

The Stranger's House

The stranger's house under the beech
is loury with verdigris summers.
The clotted path at the gable-end
is alive with the fretting of bees,
wasps in the orchard hollow pippins
that cling to cankered limbs
or rot in a tangle of nettle and dock.

Mist off the river fields shrouds
grimed-over windows.
In the gloom behind one starred pane
a mummified cat lies under the hearth,
a hagstone is nailed to the lintel,
a votive over the mantel
is snuffed by the quickening dark.

The chill in the muttering air
clings to leery wallpaper roses,
corpse-pennies blacken in clevvies
and still under the eaves is the sound
of a greenstick child, breathing
the silence that hardened
her bones to a stranger's.

Cailín Rua
(After various Old Master paintings of Mary Magdalene)

The shade of misfortune,
islanders whispered; a touch of the tinker's fire.
They kept her under the roof, for fear sun
might fan flame in her hair.
Abroad at first light, one sight of her
turned fishermen back from the shore.
Warned away from the boats,
she stripped off her homespun,
swam with the tide to the mainland,
drifted down trade winds,
discovered new worlds. At the Louvre,
Prado, Uffizi, and Pompidou,

                          she learned Magdalene too,
was a *cailín rua*; the Masters
brushed her tresses cadmium and carmine
till sparks flew — she wasn't a natural gold —
cardinals condemned
her henna-spiced hair as trademark,
like a barber's pole or usurer's golden balls.
Whore's flag, they preached. *Penitent's footwipe.*

The island woman will not be harlotized,
though the gleam of copper draws
men from Syria, Jordan and Egypt.
She lifts a gold-flecked hank off her neck
to fall with the cool rustle of barley sheaves
over speckled shoulders,
draws a twisted braid across a brow
damp with the sun's tears,

                          declines to say
if it is she, glass in hand, on the Quay d'Orsay,
or spread nude over rocks at the Hermitage,
Titian locks a cascade to her waist,
face turned away. That flame-haired *incognita*

snapped in poor light leaving a yacht at Marseille —
or arriving? The intimate shot with the Jewish host
at a farewell supper in The Upstairs Room?
No comment. A life in pictures: museworthy glimpses.
She remembers tarred currachs burning,
keeps *omerta*.

The Fisherman's Song to the Mermaid

Your brain glitters
with a madness of metals,
you're going under,

leaden boned, skull heavy
as a sunken ship's bell
crusted with echoes,

its clapper manacled.
This is no time for songs,
Sirenita mia,

mercury embolisms
stalk your green blood,
your teeth are too blunt

for the salmon hunt,
you shadow the sea-otter's wake,
scavenge his leavings,

your metal-fatigued tail-scales
tarnish and fall.
Your hair has lost its holdfast,

it floats in-shore on the tide.
Stripped of your mane,
your siren song, your shining tail,

you flail against your ebbing sea-life.
Slip-stream my bow wave,
let the green seas carry you ashore,

beach you on the high-water line
above the sandwaves.
Glean new flotsam tresses,

let *Corda filum* thongs
take root in your skull,
watered with your own green blood.

Rinse the sand from your new hair,
comb with this backbone of a Dover sole,
braid it with ribbons of sea-wrack,

stud it with whelk shells,
seahorses, starfish.
Sirenita mia, you must

fork yourself like us, like me.
Take this blue razor-shell,
slice from tail-fin to pubic bone,

cut deep, deep so I can love you.

The Dream of the Fisherman's Wife

(Katsushika Hokusai. *The Dream of the Fisherman's Wife*, woodcut c.1820)

In the dark my fisherman shapes
me, his girl-diver, to his wants,
tastes his dream-geisha,
inked teeth in her reddened *moue*,
face nightingale-shit bright,

hair a lacquered bowl, camellia-oiled.
I slip from his shingle-hard grip,
sink in the dark undersea with the octopus.
I dream Hokusai dreaming me,
a *frisson* as his paper-thin blade pares

deep into woodblock, each of us
picturing jet hair undone,
strands fish-oil glazed root to tip,
a reef-knotted waist-long cascade.
Two days have passed since I bathed;

my breasts are sweat-pearled,
ripe with aromas of *fruit de mer*.
My tentacled one unfurls, his touch
exquisite as the brush of electric eels,
his glossy fingerings on my nape

supple as young pine shoots.
The artist's chisel probes
again and again, sliver by fine sliver
till at last I am dreamed
heartwood, printed in India ink.

He hand-tints my skin
while I dream his mouth-filling tongue,
my dream of a thousand years
in colours fleet as this floating world
no fisherman comes near.

Watching Alice

Down there, Alice says,
the Borrowers are.
She shows me a miniature
family in her picture book.
Her forehead is printed
with the cracks between boards
from peering under the floor.

Cheek pressed flat
to the window-pane,
she waves across the street
to the hearse leaving her house,
the following cars, the man
in a high-viz vest
dismantling the temporary barrier.

They are the buriers, taking
granddad to live under ground.
He'll come out when he's small
and we are asleep.
She leaves him a little cake
where the skirting board
and floor don't meet.

She wants to stay up late
to see him changed to Borrower
from 'human bean'.
Someone has told her
some facts about death
but Alice is telling herself
a story she can bear.

The Snow Woman

She was a blow-in then,
the snow a wordless paper sheet,
her footprints the first blunt penstrokes
with everything still to write:
spring planting, barley sheaves,
a bitter crop of stones and chaneys
at the turn of the year.
Windblown crows dropped in
through holes punched in the sky,
gossiped year after year.
She wrote children,
they built the scarecrow in the field.

Now she's a native,
the graveyard peopled with some of her own:
a greyed husband planted these two years,
a girl half-grown,
the rest of her children flown
a thousand miles as the crow
flies from the snow-blind fields.
Silent hills shoulder her close,
crows call her name from tall trees.
She has carried the scarecrow into the house.

II. Landmarks

Walking from the Square to the West Lodge Hotel, Bantry in a Heatwave

Bluebottle summer.

Fierce heat bounces off the houses across the harbour, the pavement
      burns through my sandals.
The tide is out, fishscales and diesel shimmer on the pier.
Tied up with blue polyprop, a clinker-built wreck sinks into the slob
      under a bladder-wrack astrakhan.
Tarmac, softened to toffee, sucks at passing cars.

To my right, a hill where bullocks lumber under dusty hedgerows.
Green meadows surround the town, shadowed under ash and sycamore.
On the road out of here, crows unsettle in the crown of a beech, the
      burial ground nudges the golden strand.
The verges hum, white clover sweetens the air.

I could be home.

A Map of Getting Lost

We lean into the wind that won't let us backtrack
past the burnt-out cottage unbuilding
in the elbow of a hairpin,
render stripped back to fieldstone
like a slide of its cell structure

exposed under the sky's lens,
window frames charred and blistered.
Inside, in the stink of elder and damp cinder,
neglected swallow-nests cling to the eaves,
the roof is open to a liquorice-streaked sky.

A mark on a contour shows a headlong ravine
where a torrent, unstoppable
after this last downpour, tumbles downhill,
water quarrelling with stones.
We pretend to listen, as if going back

we might hear the wind driving us,
and not arrive as separate map-pins
pushed into hostile terrain, sharp flags snapping.
Already astray, we missed the signs
for dangerous bends and gale warnings.

New York Fire Escape

A wide-angle shot
you forgot to delete: a fan-agitated curtain
at our sixth-floor window, rooftops,
alley, the fire escape a zig-zag
of iron, crimson geraniums
against the baked wall, steps decked
with girls in crop-tops and shorts.

A frazzled mother in hitched skirts
squints into the light, fanning her breasts
and baby with a magazine.
The émigré on the landing below strokes ice
from a sweating glass over his skin.
Raucous as crows, teenage boys
on the opposite roof neck cold beers.

Your lens didn't capture the crescendo
of traffic, ghetto blasters, sirens,
the city's potpourri of deep-fried gasoline,
asphalt, dumpsters, or the child at a piano
practising, practising 'The Road out of Here'.

Since you left, the sky muffles
the sirens, crows scribble the fire-escape's
snow-clotted fretwork. Winter seeps
into the shadow-cast stairway, the cold taste
of iron sticks the tongue to the city.
Everywhere reeks of monochrome,
geranium ghosts, the silenced piano.

Traces

The crow I snatched
from an artist's fire
hangs above my desk

oil ink on heavy paper
in angled light
pencilled indentations

show traces of test crows
improperly erased
under a wax resist

careless feathers
are smashed umbrellas
hooked on city railings

the flawed beak
fixed with black acrylic
calls with the far-off

voice of crows
who ravaged crops
and fell to scattershot

their carcasses
hung in sycamores
like stinking thuribles

dispersing
warning incense
on childhood's margin.

Missing

I am in a quiet grove in a city park,
on a curved bench, in a winter night.
I am in a profile on a dating site;
in a Saturday crowd on Grafton Street;
on a midland bog; under shifting dunes;
among Sitka roots in a Wicklow wood;
in a council drain.

I am in the tramp and suck
of hiking boots on a sheep track
through a distant hill; under heather raked
flat by a Force 10; in the wind's breath;
in a still lake. I am in a Garda file;
a requiem mass; a month's mind;
the open verdict at the coroner's inquest.

I am in a glimpse from a passing truck
of letters carved on a roadside cross
at a black spot; in plastic wreaths
and ranked toy bears. I am in the SOS
cut short by wires yanked
from a phone kiosk; in the dark hour lost
when the clock goes back.

I am on weathered posters; in a snapshot
from a photo booth; in the night train's
whistle; the wind's harp-notes
in the cable stays of a Dublin bridge.
Under your forehead bone in the seahorse
coils where memory lives, whisper my name.
I have not disappeared.

Birch Tree Grove

This shelter belt
on the edge
of a Wicklow wood:
I have seen
faded photographs
of headscarved women
in a grove like this,
waiting, their backs
against winter-barked
trees, children
tucked under their coats.

On the frozen march
from the transport,
perhaps they wondered
at the absence of ice
on the black pond
behind the brick chimneys,
and the nurse trees
seemed a buffer
against rough herding
between rows
of singing wire,

a place to set down
weary bundles
and settle the children
out of the wind.

Wake
(i.m. Seamus Heaney)

I waked him in the Devil's Glen
among birch and oak above Glanmore

where his lines are chiselled on a bench.
A breeze riffled the paperback
he once signed 'fondest wishes';
his poems flowed, *a river in the trees.*

And some may call it spirit music,
wind trembling the night-ear's reed
off Blascaod Mór; some fiddlers hear
a *caoineadh*, name it 'Port na Sídhe'.

The brave row out past the islands,
hear wave-tunes whistled from rain
or the keening of the shearwater,
a soulbird singing home.

There's always a song on the wind,
if only we are still and tune our ears,
even the grave sings memory, the dead
poet lives in all he wrote and said.

Inheritors

"What thou lov'st well is thy true heritage." — Ezra Pound, The *Cantos*.

We could show you the holt
where the otter lies up,
we could show you his run,
his fishbony spraint,
but we won't: we keep *schtum*

where the old trout waits out the heat
under the bank, a five pounder
wise to the ways of the rod man
stood hours in his rubbers
out in the channel,

up to his tricks with iron blue
and stonefly, taking a dozen
brown trout on the fly,
hooked, played, landed,
trapped in a keep-net,

weighed, ogled, photographed,
set back in the water air-stunned,
barely alive, to survive if they can.
You won't find us in the *Angling Times*
waving our first-of-the-season.

We reckon weight by girth. Tiddlers
go over the side for heron and otter.
Our keepers are head-to-tail muscle
like a man's thigh. A smack of the priest
stops them drowning in air.

From the wooden bridge at Fiddown
to the stone span at Kilsheelan,
this river is ours, our veins
run blue with her water.
We're tied to Suir tides,

up before dawn, out in our boots,
blowing our nails, shooting nets
on our stretch of pigeon-grey water,
minding no bye-laws, no quotas:
taking what's wild is not thieving.

We pay our dues
in bronchial coughs and rheumatics,
in rescues and drownings.
We know the currents, we're there
when the bodies surface.

We know the channels and runnels,
the cuts and eddies and undertows.
Our slim double-ender glides
where the river spreads thin
as a silk slip past the sally islands.

The cot handles light; built
for this old, slow water, she draws
less than a swan.
We know the mudbanks, we've seen
men sink in the stink,

so we step light where the tide
leaves the slob muscled and ridged.
We haul up out of sight
of the bailiff, give him the slip
on the backroads,

headlights switched off
and the boot scraping the tarmac,
weighed down with salmon and grilse
shiny as tin, packed head to tail.
If some four-star chef doesn't ask

for our tags, we let him haggle us down
to the price in our heads.
Let twisted writs call us outlaws,
we're common-law heirs
to boatmen, stroke haulers,

snap-netters, our line
reaches back before Cromwell.
We claim our birthright
with double-wound snare,
with gaff-hook and snap-net.

We take our young in the cot,
show them what's theirs,
teach them the patience of herons,
the stealth of the rat,
the speed of the otter,

how to ambush a two-winter salmon
and tickle a trout till he's drowsy,
then, quick as eels,
hook a thumb through his gills
and land him in the pan for supper.

They'll know the kingfisher's burrow,
the shoals of horsehair-thin elvers
wriggling upstream, the strong
silver-quick eels setting out
on the 6000 miles to Sargasso.

We'll dawdle downriver,
find a spot to haul up in the shade,
pluck a lapful of holes from the air,
knot them together to make
nets to go fishing, come Monday.

Landmarks

I walked the farm from the road back to the bounds,
saw night draw down, a gentle dark surround fields
I'd hoped to find unchanged by absent years.

Here, Grandfather lit fires to split hell-hot rock,
built drystone walls, clay-mortared gaps
and hauled manure by horse-drawn cart
to coax yellow clay to yield crops
of oats, barley, *British Queens* and mangolds.

Then Father in his day packed gelignite into holes
drilled into the outcrop, lit the fuse.
We children ran like rabbits for the calf shed
while blasted rocks bombarded the tin roof
and the smallest child howled.

His life was war waged on limestone that broke
through his small ocean of mean, misshapen fields
like a whale's head and fluke, creviced and blue.
He chased his dream of lush grass on stony ground,
pushed an inconvenient *lios* into a cairn with a JCB.

This dusk, I walked alone through history
coded in field names: *Bun na hInse, Bán Lisín*,
rushy *Mainteán Giabach*. Past *Bán Carraigeach*
the ancient furze horse-pasture is bare sward,
a thin grass quilt spread on knees of broken rock.

In place of woods, I found a view wide open,
clear to Slievenamon, a farm of broad paddocks,
just as my father dreamed; razed hedge-scars healed,
Gaelic field names erased, with what they mean.
The past is near the surface, its pulse is under my feet.

Miracle
(A reflection on Littlewood's Law of Miracles)

Littlewood's law states what we call miracles
are merely happenings of some significance
which everyone encounters once a month;
a one per million chance. Or so says science,
but let me put a case for the reverse:
a blind man with a chainsaw hired to slash
the heavy lower branches from our ash.
Each day he leaned his white cane on our fence,
then fingertipped to read both girth and bark,
while we kept distant from his chainsaw's roar.
He lopped and logged, despite his inner dark,
and when he'd worked a month, we gathered up
the logs he'd cut. All ash. No beech or oak, no bone
or flesh. And that was miracle enough.

Grushie

The rain has stopped. Sunlight
veneers a table set between windows.
The year turns.
To the south: a window half-filled
with pewter lake topped with pine and naked sky.
The window to the west leans out to frame
a pair of toxic yews, the native kind.
A foal-at-heel runs to brood mares grazing the field.
Its pliant hooves drum light as raindrops.

Behind the house, men clear herbaceous borders,
burn snapdragons and red hot pokers,
the acrid tang of bonfire clings to scarred thornproofs.
A gravelled path munches boots.
In jeans and scarlet gansey, a woman
rakes leaves into drifts she shovels
onto a rust-scabbed wheelbarrow.
The rake's tines are worn to stubs,
its beech handle slips through her palms,
polished by generations of hands.
She barrows leaves over a weathered oak plank
to the fire on the kitchen-garden terrace.

At the bottom of a steep slope
a wooden boathouse stands at the water's edge,
glazed black and reeking of creosote.

A pontoon of oil drums floats on the cold flat lake.
Here all is motionless: air, pontoon, water,
the far shore's fringe of yellowed spruce,
its reflection.
Below the surface, invisible pike hang suspended.
It is like winter: still, cold, relentless.
It is like death.

Near the house, at the top of the slope,
the season turns. The wind burns,
woods blaze to burnt sugar and molten jazz.
Beech and birch broadcast pale coins
across the shivery grass.
They dull to tarnished brass
the way a grushie flung from chapel steps
is diminished
by the splendour of the bride.

From Céide Fields:

(i) Stone Song

The iron probe
strikes a capstone
on a muffled wall

under the bog
the stone sings
down 5000 years

a ringing note
old as anvil music
Goibhniu forged

or talking drums
on mesolithic hills
a spark-bright sound

sprung from the dark
combines with far-off
children chanting

skipping rhymes
under a Belmullet
street light.

(ii) The Inkling

That first time it breathed a sigh on your neck.
Why did you brush it aside?
You should have taken it into your head.

There was still time to build it a shrine,
offer crowberry prayers and top-of-the-milk.
White breath hung over the cattle-pens.

You carried on felling and burning,
spread baskets of kelp and sand on the land.
The inkling shivered your spine.

Did it come from the ocean?
It lurked in the mizzle, blackened the haws,
wormed down to your worrybone.

Years have gone by. The cradles lie empty.
Summer is wetter than winter.
Rain drenches the land. It quenches the sky.

You break the skin on the earth with your *sleán,*
drive the blade deep with your foot.
Bogwater wells from the wound.

Grass lies down in the fields and drowns.
Cattle bawl their hunger pains.
There is only one child in the house.

You can't shake the inkling.
It niggles, raises the back of your hair,
sly and fat as a tick.

Barley decays in the ground.

The cow is near dry. You must choose
between calf and child.

It is out of your hands.

(iii) Becoming the Ancestor

As in prehistory a woman
        climbed down these wave-fretted
                cliffs and stretched to rest
                        on this shore,

so lay your cheek
        on this time-worn stone
                and, looking north
                        along longitude 9

to where the blue wind
        splits sea from sky,
                follow its trajectory
                        from that birthing point

to your curious eye;
        so learn, as she may have done,
                how this earth curves,
                    and time.

(iv) The Laying of the Bog

She spun her warp-thread from the salt Atlantic,
her weft was bog-bean, myrtle, asphodel,
Earth wove herself a bog as comfort blanket,
sphagnum and bog-cotton layered her quilt.

Purple moor-grass was her needle; she embroidered
a curse cross-stitched in threads of twisted rain,
grey skies, false dawns and thunder. She remembered
how farmers burned her cloak of oak and pine.

She spread her hex-cloth as a wild-hued grave for men
who circled stones as walls to hold their kin
and cattle safe from winter's wuthering
under scraw thatch where no sky came in.

Beneath Earth's coverlet of marled tweed
lie bones of smothered farms and drowned fields.

(v) South of Erris

The anvil cloud ruptured,
lightning tore the sky,
its sound like ripping silk.

Between crash and flash
we searched the pipeline
for signs of explosion.

Someone said the musket shot
that felled the last wolf hereabouts
cracked sharp as thunder.

After the country
we had driven through,
a place shaped by mourning,

the white feather and down
of our five star hotel
didn't sit well with us.

Double-glazed against the rain
dissolving our reflections,
I don't think we had much to say.

Homecoming

I'm driving home
through a moth-storm,
powdery drifts bank
on the windshield,
the windows are down,
the air mushroomy
with August heat.

I'll call again
from a mile out.
Wait under the porch lamp
for my headlights
to crest the hill,
for the car to turn at last
onto the home stretch...

In the morning dark
before you know
I'll take the first mushroom
new sprung
from the humid night,
white, fat-tipped, eager
for my fingers.

Haiku Sequence from The Farmhouse, Wicklow

The year's first frost sweetening the sloes

tangled
in blue fescue grass
a pigeon feather

turning from blue to winter green the last hydrangea

starlings feast
on shrivelled birdcherries —
petrol vapour shimmers

a vixen's scream…
the hills darken
against the night sky

chainsaw
in the half-dark —
brilliant blue sparks

winter logs
stacked in the zinc shed…
night creatures rustle

chimney smoke
reeling in
the full moon

Horse Stance

I mean to leave
before night draws in
and photo-sensors trigger
the lights along the N11.
I mean to drive away
from the sloping field
where the brood mare
braces her hindquarters
and pours her yellow stream
onto the autumn grass.

Precision-balanced
on flexed hindquarters,
she is facing down
a ground invasion
of oncoming pylons
advancing high-tension cables
across the Wicklow hills,
standing her ground
against thrumming air
in a cloud of her own steam.

I mean to leave
before they take all her sky.

If What is, is Other
(After Pablo Neruda, *The Book of Questions*)

Is it the taint of cracked milk on marble?
      A cat's mangy caress on an ankle?
I have tasted the clean rustle of barley straw
      where the crow's fetor soaks
             the fertile earth.

Unless it's a slip of velvet lining a pocket?
      A beach pebble set in a 24 carat platinum ring?
I have felt a cello's strings move air in my brain,
      tasted in half-light its fumes like single malt,
           the last drops.

Could it be that first formless shriek of a newborn?
      The trembling of wind in a cave of singing ice?
I have touched the sea's breath among mountain pine,
      heard clover dying in the silence
           of wild bees.

Perhaps it is the thud of a frozen goldcrest striking the ground?
      A pilot whale's vertebrae on a cottage lawn?
I have tasted spring rain in a fistful of ripe corn,
      felt a nocturne in a dark wood,
           the deepest shade.

Or is it the fizz between the idea and its orbit?
      A nerve's flash like lightning splitting a bone?
I have breathed enigmas, seen cryptic echoes leap
      the steep cliffs of the skull.
           I understand nothing.

Tremolo

Crossing a bog, do not measure progress
in pitfalls, let your eye be your compass,
needle fixed on a floating point lined up
with some heather clump or blasted tree.
Pace the journey to the heart's tempo,
its metered beat steadies the quaking terrain,
your claggy footfalls damp its vibrations.

Take this much on trust: behind you,
the slow curve of foot-shaped depressions,
insects treading a boghole's teeming skin.
As the path becomes memory, the history
of the future is woven in peat.
Above you always, a lark; its trembling note
pours down like raindrops.

Glimpsed

In sunlit bracken
on a forest margin,
three young stoats
gyrated, white-bibbed,
sleek-headed,
with the soot-tipped tails
that stay when winter turns
summer coats to ermine.

They purled in mad,
fantastic-cabled whirligigs,
spun to the fiddling
worm in the brain,
as if illuminations shaped
in ancient scriptoria
had slipped the scribe's hand
and, conjured to full blood,

danced for the span
of a grasshopper's song,
then vanished in a finger-snap,
but glimpsed again
among the velum pages
of *The Book of Kells*:
stoat spirits racing
along lines of text
or puzzled into Celtic knots.

Silver Birches

(*Finnbhean na Coille*. Fair woman of the woods /Silver Birch)

Once they were sap-sweet
and green; they knew nothing of time,
how it spirals faster and faster.
They stood by the pathway
shaking their sequins,
a silvery sound like the tinkle of ferret-bells,

or they tilted their heads,
arms arched for a half-pirouette;
miniscule movements
compared to the flight of a bird or a fly,
yet they learned the sky,
learned the disturbance of air, quartered the year.

The greening circled,
strings of new beads dangled from fingertips
freshly erupted from last season's knuckles;
abundant new tresses,
new green-spangled dresses.

New losses.

Hardened by the judgement of cold,
stripped of their hair
and coin-trimmed clothes,
they spinney themselves,
raise a coppice to lean on,

a coven of silver birches
showing their bones,
skin curled at the edges,
bark vellum an exile might peel with a penknife
to write a gulag of poems
with charcoals of burnt bone.

They imitate rain.
They know all that there is to know:
what grass is, and stars;
that dreams are leaves;
each frozen flake is a syllable snow slots into silence.
They know all the words for winter.

Naming the Boat

In his dream the woman is hazy, robin's egg blue,
almost transparent, hovering over the river,
not speaking, leaving him cold as winter and blue.
He's stirring paint-dregs together, naming the blues:
rainwashed, midnight, salmon-back, tidal water.
On the radio 'Lady Sings the Blues',
the singer's voice the precise cloudwater blue
his spirit-woman wants him to paint her name
on the bow of the boat he has never named,
knowing a named boat takes a human soul, blue
as water, the soul of one who has gone
in the river. The river is calling his lover to go

to her drowning, its sleepless trickle whispers, *Go!*
in her ear all the unbearable midnight-blue
hours, waterwords tricking her. It's time to go
night-fishing. Can he know, yet not know, she'll go
out of her head while he's out on the river,
sifting water through nets where wild salmon go
contra-flow? The toss of a dream-coin decides: go.
He leaves the woman who is winter water,
the long bones under her skin thinning to water.
He turns from her grey illegible already-gone-
away eyes. He dreams footsteps, calls her name,
hears only a patter of raindrops naming

each leaf: hazel, birch, alder, ash, names
shivery as light on water. He goes
where the watersong calls, this man named
before birth for a river, his name
more than a name. Clear as dragonfly blue
wings spell summer, he hears their names
in the pitter of rain on water, the naming-
spell he heard the first day he sat, feet in the river
next to his lover's. Leaves dream-fall on the river,

the quicken is dropping its berries, the name-
spell is turning the flow of Anner Water.
And Suir, a woman essential as water,

is fading, dissolving like waterlogged paper, bleeding loops of her name
into factory runoff — water
the scientists claim is sweet water,
pure as the rain that falls where clouds go
over the Gulf Stream. The dreamer sees red water-
spiderlings hatch from the eggs of a water-
hen. The legs of the patient blue
heron are scald-marked and eaten. Blue
tinges the morning mist shrouding the water;
night-fog like mourning-crepe drapes over the river;
crows dive from the trees and swim in the river,

all omens that something's awry with the river
that feeds the town reservoir. Craving water,
the woman drains glass after glass of the river.
It leaches her spirit, she's waning, the river's
dissolving the strength in her name,
scarring her bones with a rune for *lost river.*
Sealing her fate, water-fowl leave the river,
arrow its banks with claw-marks that tell her *go
to the drowning.* The dreaming man sees her go
glassy-eyed, gauzy as vapour, sees the river
possess her, flow into her faded blue
veins, turning their cobwebby map river-blue.

Suir Lady Sings the Blues in cloudwater blue
on the bow of a boat filled with river-
smooth boulders, lying low in water
up to the lines of her name, the naming
spelling a soul into the boat, letting her go.

Summer's End

Inside the Clip 'n' Dye
the barber shears sunblond locks
from two tow-headed boys.

In rhythmic swing, the apprentice sweeps
drifts of shorn hair that fall light
as hay-swathes round the chair,

the way we used to fork the mow
into long hot windrows
left to bake a day under a sun

that seems always to have burned
high above the stubble, a spur
to our steady toss-and-turn,

tedding toward the gallon tin
sweating in its headland tent
of cool green stems

at the meadow's shady end.
We shivered at its slaking chill,
heads thrown back, throats working

to swallow greedy gulps, overspill
running over sunburned shoulders,
wishing summer's labours over.

Finished, the barber shakes
the gleanings off the cape,
angles a mirror for a backward glimpse

of stubbled scalp, ring of tender neck,
a pale half-moon above the ears
and all of summer on the floor.

The Furnock

Even now I go there in my head,
to the furthest point on the farm.
I climb the blue limestone.
Too smooth for shoes,
it needs the toe-hold of bare feet.

It's a whale of a rock, broaching
deep in furze where Irish Draughts graze,
its skin a criss-cross of fissures
where trefoils cling, and violets,
stonecrop squishes under my toes.
And always, the shushing wind
wafts spruce, larch and Scots pine.

Seven miles off at Rathgormack
the chapel bell sounds noon,
Duggan's bullocks bawl in hungry grass,
a goods train rushing through Carrick
whistles three crow-miles from here.

Winter grass is sharp in my nostrils,
and bracken's bitter smell,
or summer hay hums with bees
and the baking-bread-and-coconut
of scorched earth and gorse.
Birdsong rains down
on cocksfoot and clover.

Leaving's like wrenching a bone.
I look back, once, from the gate;
the rock sinks into its yellow ocean,
waves of forest break behind,
Coum Seangán brightens after rain.

BREDA WALL RYAN grew up on a farm in County Waterford and now lives in County Wicklow. She has a B.A. in English and Spanish from UCC; a Post-graduate Diploma in Teaching English as a Second or Other Language from Trinity College, London; and an M.Phil. in Creative Writing (Distinction) from Trinity College, Dublin. Her awarded fiction has appeared in *The Stinging Fly*, *The Faber Book of Best New Irish Short Stories 2006-7* and *The New Hennessy Book of Irish Fiction*. Her poems have been published in *Skylight 47*, *Ink Sweat and Tears*, *Deep Water Literary Journal*, *And Other Poems*, *Fish Anthology*, *The Ofi Press*, *Orbis*, *Magma* and *The Rialto*. In 2013 Breda won the iYeats Poetry Competition, Poets Meet Painters, Dromineer Poetry Competition and Over the Edge New Writer of the Year Competition. She was selected for the Poetry Ireland Introductions Series, 2014, was awarded Second Place in the Patrick Kavanagh Awards, Third Prize in The Rialto/RSPB Nature Poetry Competition, was shortlisted for a Bridport Prize and Highly Commended in Fool for Poetry Chapbook Competition. A Pushcart Prize and Forward Prize nominee, she won the Gregory O'Donoghue International Poetry Competition, 2015.